Documents for Democracy

Building America and Literacy Skills Through Primary Sources

Volume 2: 19th Century

Prepared by
Veronica Burchard
Illustrations by Courtney Burrough

*Dedicated to my loving husband,
Kyle Burchard,
as well as my mentor and friend,
Claire McCaffery Griffin*

Unless otherwise noted, no part of this publication
may be reproduced, stored, sourced off for use in
other publications, or transmitted, in any form or by
any means, electronic, mechanical, photocopying,
recording or otherwise, without the prior written
permission of the American Institute
for History Education.

Edited by Matthew F. Galella
Design and typography by Graham Communications

Copyright © 2010 American Institute for History Education
All rights reserved

ISBN-13: 978-0-9826244-0-1

Printed in the United States of America
February 2010

Visit **www.aihe-bookstore.com**

Table of Contents

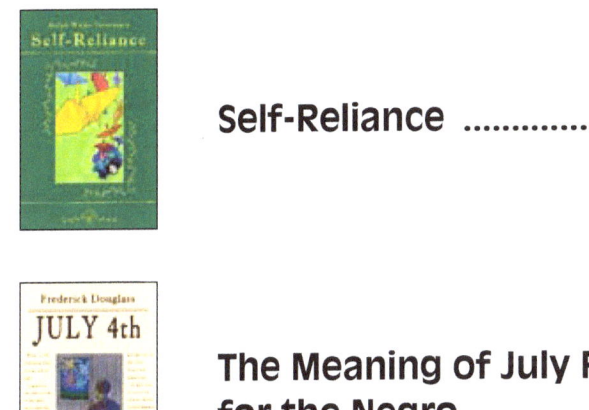

Self-Reliance 3

The Meaning of July Fourth
for the Negro 15

The Gettysburg
Address 27

The New Colossus 39

About the Author 50

Ralph Waldo Emerson's
Self-Reliance

Introduction

Ralph Waldo Emerson was a writer, speaker, and philosopher. He also served as a Unitarian minister for several years. Although he was a minister, Emerson began to feel that organized religion was not helpful to people. People needed to trust their own thoughts and feelings, rather than what their church told them. Only then would they find the truth. This belief was called "transcendentalism."

Ralph Waldo Emerson

At the core of transcendentalism was belief in oneself. Emerson thought people should be true to themselves, and have faith in their own minds. They should not just try to do what they have seen others do; nor should they only repeat what they have heard others say.

Emerson explained his philosophy in his essay *Self-Reliance*. It was published in 1841. At the time, Emerson's ideas were very new and even scary to many people. But they caught on. Emerson helped build the idea of American individualism.

What Is a Primary Source?

A primary source is a piece of history. It is an artifact from a time period, like a diary, a speech, a newspaper article, or a photograph. In this chapter, you will study the essay *Self-Reliance* as a primary source from 1841, as a way to learn about that time period of American history.

Activating Prior Knowledge: Questions for Pre-Reading Discussion

1. What types of activities are you really good at?
2. How did you discover you had these talents?
3. What do you think is the best way to develop your talents?
4. Have you ever tried a new activity and found you had no interest in it?
5. What do you think of when you hear the phrase "self-reliance"?
6. Who do you "rely" on in your life?
7. What are some ways you rely on yourself?

Vocabulary and Context Questions

Complete this page as you read. Using context clues and/or a dictionary, define each word:

Vocabulary

reliance:

insist:

imitate:

cultivation:

adopted:

possession:

exhibited:

unique:

assigned

Context Questions

1. Who wrote this essay?
2. When did he write it?
3. What was his purpose?
4. Who read this essay?

Insist on yourself; never imitate.

Your own gift you can present every moment with the force of a whole life's cultivation; but of the adopted talent of another, you have only half possession.

That which each can do best, none but his Maker can teach him. No man yet knows what it is, nor can, till that person has exhibited it.

Where is the master who could have taught Shakespeare? Where is the master who could have instructed Franklin, or Washington, or Bacon, or Newton?

Every great man is unique.

Shakespeare will never be made by the study of Shakespeare.

Do that which is assigned you, and you cannot hope too much or dare too much.

Self-Reliance

Insist on yourself; never imitate.

Your own gift you can present every moment
with the force of a whole life's cultivation;

but of the adopted talent of another,
you have only half possession.

That which each can do best,
none but his Maker can teach him.

No man yet knows what it is, nor can,
till that person has exhibited it.

Where is the master who could have
taught Shakespeare?

Where is the master who could have instructed
Franklin, or Washington, or Bacon, or Newton?

Every great man is unique.

Shakespeare will never be made
by the study of Shakespeare.

Do that which is assigned you,
and you cannot hope too much or dare too much.

Frederick Douglass

JULY 4th

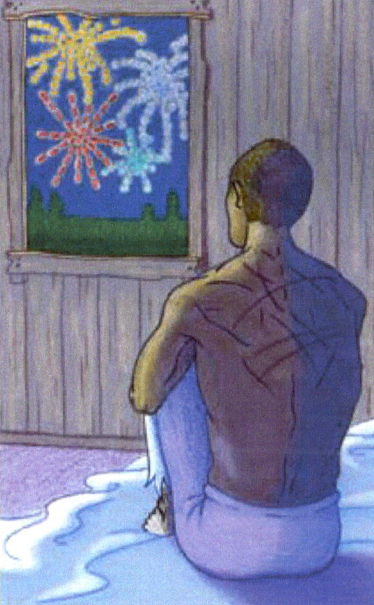

What, to the American slave, is your 4th of July?

I answer; a day that reveals to the slave, more than any all other days in the year, the gross injustice and cruelty to which he is the constant victim.

To him, your celebration is a sham: your nat--ional greatness, swelling vanity; Your sounds of rejoicing are empty and heart--less; your shout of liberty and equality, hollow mockery;

Your prayers and hymns, your sermons and thanks-givings are to the slave, fraud and hypocrisy.

A thin veil to cover up crimes which would disgrace a nation of savages.

There is not a nation on the earth guilty of prac--tices more shocking and bloody than are the people of the United States at this

Introduction

Frederick Douglass was born a slave in Maryland. He escaped in 1838, and traveled to freedom in New York. He soon joined with other people who were working to end slavery in the United States. Fighting for equality became his life's work.

Frederick Douglass

When he was 23, Douglass gave his first speech. He was a great speaker and impressed many in the audience. He was soon asked to give a series of lectures on slavery. Douglass wrote a book, published a newspaper, and continued speaking out about why slavery was wrong.

On July 5, 1852, Douglass spoke to a crowd in Rochester, New York. It was the day after Independence Day. Douglass believed that it was not right for Americans to celebrate their freedom when American slaves had no freedom. He decided to make his speech about what the Fourth of July meant to a slave. He hoped to encourage more Americans to work to end slavery.

Douglass lived to see slavery banned in the United States in 1865. He had worked his entire life for that goal and for the equality of all people.

What Is a Primary Source?

A primary source is a piece of history. It is an artifact from a time period, like a diary, a speech, a newspaper article, or a photograph. In this chapter, you will study the speech *The Meaning of July Fourth for the Negro* as a primary source from 1852, as a way to learn about that time period of American history.

Activating Prior Knowledge: Questions for Pre-Reading Discussion

1. Why do Americans celebrate the Fourth of July?
2. What do you think are the best things about that holiday?
3. Have you heard of Frederick Douglass? What do you know about him?
4. What do you know about the history of slavery in the United States?
5. How do you think slaves felt when whites celebrated the Fourth of July?

Vocabulary and Context Questions

Complete this page as you read. Using context clues and/or a dictionary, define each word:

Vocabulary

gross:

injustice:

sham:

liberty:

hollow:

mockery:

fraud:

hypocrisy:

despair:

doom:

Context Questions

1. Who wrote this speech?
2. When did he write it?
3. What was his purpose?
4. Who heard or read this speech?

What, to the American slave, is your Fourth of July?

I answer; a day that reveals to the slave, more than all other days in the year, the gross injustice and cruelty to which he is the constant victim.

To him, your celebration is a sham; your national greatness, swelling vanity.

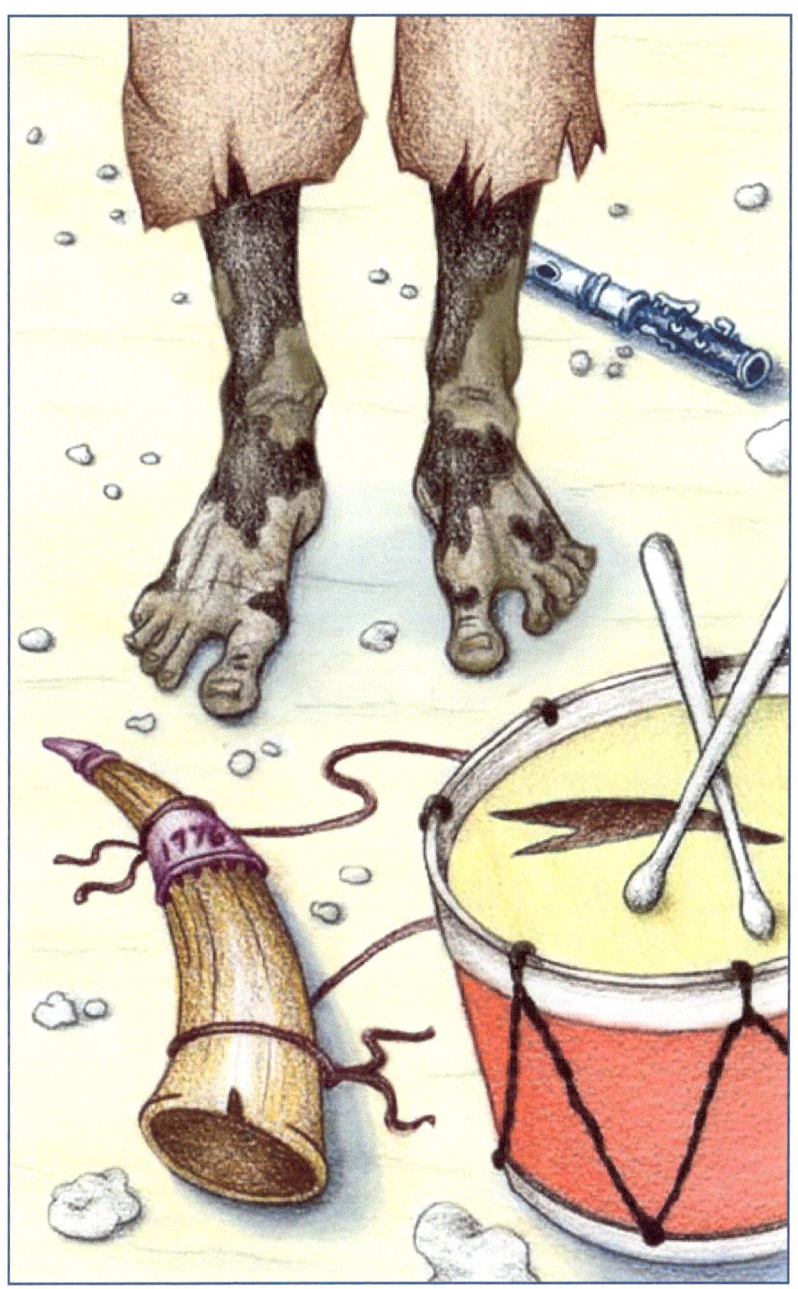

Your sounds of rejoicing are empty and heartless;
your shout of liberty and equality, hollow mockery.

Your prayers and hymns, your sermons and thanksgivings are to the slave, fraud and hypocrisy. A thin veil to cover up crimes which would disgrace a nation of savages.

There is not a nation on the earth guilty of practices more shocking and bloody than are the people of the United States, at this very hour.

[But] I do not despair of this country. There are forces which must work the downfall of slavery. "The arm of the Lord is not shortened," and the doom of slavery is certain.

The Meaning of July Fourth for the Negro

What, to the American slave, is your Fourth of July?

I answer; a day that reveals to the slave,
more than all other days in the year,
the gross injustice and cruelty to which
he is the constant victim.

To him, your celebration is a sham;
your national greatness, swelling vanity.
Your sounds of rejoicing are empty and heartless;
your shout of liberty and equality, hollow mockery.

Your prayers and hymns,
your sermons and thanks-givings
are to the slave, fraud and hypocrisy.

A thin veil to cover up crimes
which would disgrace a nation of savages.
There is not a nation on the earth guilty of practices
more shocking and bloody than are the people of
the United States, at this very hour.

[But] I do not despair of this country. There are
forces which must work the downfall of slavery.

"The arm of the Lord is not shortened,"
and the doom of slavery is certain.

The Gettysburg Address

Four score and seven years ago our fathers brought forth, on this continent, a new nation...

Introduction

One of the bloodiest battles of the Civil War was the Battle of Gettysburg. An estimated 8,000 men were killed during that three-day battle, which took place in July 1863. Altogether there were about 51,000 total casualties that included soldiers killed, wounded, captured or missing. When the Union troops won, the battle was over, but the war went on.

Abraham Lincoln

It was time to bury the dead, and plans were made for a National Cemetery. President Abraham Lincoln was invited to Gettysburg, Pennsylvania, to give a speech at the dedication of the cemetery. President Lincoln wanted to honor the Union soldiers who had fought and died at Gettysburg. But he also had another purpose. He wanted to give new meaning to the soldiers' sacrifice.

Until then, Lincoln had always said the purpose of the Civil War was to save the Union. While giving the speech — called the *Gettysburg Address* — on November 19, 1863, Lincoln said the purpose of the Civil War was to end slavery in the United States. Of even greater importance, Lincoln explained that if the United States was going to live up to its ideals, slavery would have to end.

What Is a Primary Source?

A primary source is a piece of history. It is an artifact from a time period, like a diary, a speech, a newspaper article, or a photograph. In this chapter, you will study the speech the *Gettysburg Address* as a primary source from 1863, as a way to learn about that time period of American history.

Activating Prior Knowledge: Questions for Pre-Reading Discussion

1. What do you know about the Civil War?
2. What do you know about Abraham Lincoln? Can you list some of his most important achievements as President of the United States?
3. What do you know about the history of slavery in the United States?
4. Have you ever heard the phrase "actions speak louder than words"? What does it mean? Do you agree?
5. Abraham Lincoln wanted to encourage Americans to live up to the country's ideals. What are some of those?
6. How do you live up to American ideals in your own life?

Vocabulary and Context Questions

Complete this page as you read. Using context clues and/or a dictionary, define each word:

Vocabulary

score:

conceived:

liberty:

dedicated:

proposition:

endure:

advanced:

resolve:

in vain:

perish

Context Questions

1. Who wrote this speech?
2. When did he write it?
3. What was his purpose?
4. Who heard or read the *Gettysburg Address*?

Four score and seven years ago our fathers brought forth on this continent a new nation,

conceived in Liberty, and dedicated to the proposition that all men are created equal.

Now we are engaged in a great civil war, testing whether that nation, or any nation, so conceived and so dedicated, can long endure.

We are met on a great battle-field of that war. We have come to dedicate a portion of that field, as a final resting place for those who here gave their lives that that nation might live.

The world will little note, nor long remember what we say here, but it can never forget what they did here. It is for us the living, rather, to be dedicated here to the unfinished work which they who fought here have advanced.

We here highly resolve that these dead shall not have died in vain — that this nation, under God, shall have a new birth of freedom,

and that government of the people, by the people, for the people, shall not perish from the earth.

The Gettysburg Address

Four score and seven years ago
our fathers brought forth
on this continent a new nation,
conceived in Liberty, and dedicated
to the proposition that all men are created equal.

Now we are engaged in a great civil war,
testing whether that nation, or any nation,
so conceived and so dedicated, can long endure.

We are met on a great battle-field of that war.
We have come to dedicate a portion of that field,
as a final resting place for those
who here gave their lives that that nation might live.

The world will little note, nor long remember
what we say here,
but it can never forget what they did here.

It is for us the living, rather,
to be dedicated here to the unfinished work
which they who fought here have advanced.

We here highly resolve that these dead shall not
have died in vain — that this nation, under God, shall
have a new birth of freedom,

and that government of the people, by the people,
for the people, shall not perish from the earth.

Introduction

In 1883, a New York City poet named Emma Lazarus was asked to write a poem for a new statue that France was going to give to the United States. It was going to be called the Statue of Liberty, and it would be placed in New York Harbor. Lazarus wrote a poem called *The New Colossus*, and donated it to help raise money for the statue's pedestal.

Emma Lazarus

In the 1800s, people continued to come to the United States as they had since the early 1600s. These waves of immigrants included European Jews, Irish Catholics, Italians, Poles, Germans, and members of many other groups. They made up the "melting pot" of America. These immigrants often came to America through New York Harbor. When they arrived, the first glimpse of America they saw was often the Statue of Liberty.

Lazarus' poem helped define Lady Liberty. The poem even changed the way people thought of liberty itself. Liberty was not something that Americans got once and for all in 1776. Liberty was something people all over the world were seeking. They came to America to find it. The Statue of Liberty has welcomed immigrants to the United States for more than one hundred years.

What Is a Primary Source?

A primary source is a piece of history. It is an artifact from a time period, like a diary, a speech, a newspaper article, or a photograph. In this chapter, you will study the poem *The New Colossus* as a primary source from 1883, as a way to learn about that time period of American history.

Activating Prior Knowledge: Questions for Pre-Reading Discussion

1. Have you ever seen the Statue of Liberty? In photographs? Or in person?
2. When did your family come to the United States?
3. Did you know the Statue of Liberty has a poem on the pedestal?
4. If you had to guess, what do you think that poem might be about?
5. How do you think immigrants felt (and feel) when they arrived in New York Harbor and saw the Statue of Liberty?
6. Have you ever heard the United States' motto, "*e Pluribus Unum*"? What does it mean?

Vocabulary and Context Questions

Complete this page as you read. Using context clues and/or a dictionary, define each word:

Vocabulary

colossus:

brazen:

conquering:

mighty:

imprisoned:

exiles:

beacon:

storied pomp:

yearning:

wretched:

tempest:

Context Questions

1. Who wrote this poem?
2. When did she write it?
3. What was her purpose?
4. Who heard or read this poem?

Not like the brazen giant of Greek fame,
With conquering limbs astride from land to land;

Here at our sea-washed, sunset gates shall stand
A mighty woman

With a torch, whose flame
Is the imprisoned lightning, and her name
Mother of Exiles.

From her beacon-hand
Glows world-wide welcome;

Her mild eyes command
The air-bridged harbor that twin cities frame.
"Keep, ancient lands, your storied pomp!" cries she
With silent lips.

"Give me your tired, your poor,
Your huddled masses yearning to breathe free,
The wretched refuse of your teeming shore.
Send these, the homeless, tempest-tost to me,

I lift my lamp beside the golden door!"

The New Colossus

Not like the brazen giant of Greek fame,

With conquering limbs astride from land to land;

Here at our sea-washed, sunset gates shall stand

A mighty woman with a torch, whose flame

Is the imprisoned lightning, and her name

Mother of Exiles. From her beacon-hand

Glows world-wide welcome; her mild eyes command

The air-bridged harbor that twin cities frame.

"Keep, ancient lands, your storied pomp!" cries she

With silent lips. "Give me your tired, your poor,

Your huddled masses yearning to breathe free,

The wretched refuse of your teeming shore.

Send these, the homeless, tempest-tost to me,

I lift my lamp beside the golden door!"

About the Author

After teaching for seven years, Veronica Burchard became the Director of Curriculum Development for an educational nonprofit organization near Washington, D.C. She earned her bachelor's and master's degrees in English from the University of Florida, and her interests include American literature and civic education. Veronica lives with her husband, two sons and a very hungry guinea pig in Fairfax, Virginia.

www.ingramcontent.com/pod-product-compliance
Lightning Source LLC
Chambersburg PA
CBHW041526090426
42736CB00035B/23